EARTH IN DANGER!

Farming

Polly Goodman

HODDER
Wayland

an imprint of Hodder Children's Books

Titles in the **EARTH IN DANGER!** series

Coasts	Rivers
Energy	Settlements
Farming	Transport

For more information on this series and other Hodder Wayland titles, go to www.hodderwayland.co.uk

This book is a simplified version of the title *Farming* in Hodder Wayland's 'Earth Alert' series.

Language level consultant: Norah Granger
Editor: Belinda Hollyer
Designer: Jane Hawkins

First published in 2001 by Hodder Wayland,
an imprint of Hodder Children's Books.

This paperback edition published in 2005

Britian Library Cataloguing in Publication Data
Goodman, Polly
Farming. - (Earth in danger!)
1. Agriculture - environmental aspects - Juvenile literature
I.Title
333.7'6
ISBN 0 7502 4726 6

Printed in China by WKT Company Limited

Hodder Children's Books
A division of Hodder Headline Limited
338 Euston Road, London NW1 3BH

Picture acknowledgements
Cover: main picture Klein/Hubert-BIOS/Still Pictures, hens Hodder Wayland Picture Library; Birdlife International (Mark Edwards) 10; Chapel Studios (Zul Mukhida) 23; Ecoscene (David Wootton) 7; Eye Ubiquitous (Chloe Johnson) 5 top, (Skjold) 9, (D. Gill) 15, (Jill Hazel) 28; Getty Images (Zane Williams) 1, (Jon Gray) 4, (Andy Sacks) 6, (Gary John Norman) 10, (David Hiser) 14, (Gary Irving) 18, (David Joel) 22, (Siegried Eigstler) 25, (Brian Atkinson) 26; Hodder Wayland Picture Library 3, 5 (bottom), 24, Impact Photos (Jorn Stjerneklar) 8, (Jorn Stjerneklar) 11, (Christine Bluntzer) 12, (Rhonda Klevansky) 13, (David Reed) 19, (Mike McQueen) 20, (Rachel Morton) 27; Margot Richardson 21(both).
Artwork by Peter Bull Art Studio.

Contents

What is farming?

Farming is the production of food and other materials by raising plants and animals. Today, many people buy their food in supermarkets close to their homes. But the food comes from many different countries and is farmed in different ways.

The way food is farmed affects the environment. It also affects people's health and the treatment of animals. Some farming methods are more harmful than others.

Apples in a supermarket can come from many different countries. ▼

In this book you can find out about food farming today, and what you can do to help protect the environment, people's health and animal welfare.

History of farming

Over 11,000 years ago, people got all their food by gathering wild plants, hunting and fishing. They wandered from place to place, moving constantly in the search for food.

But then, about 11,000 years ago, people learned how to grow plants from seeds. They learned how to raise animals. They settled in one place so they could wait for the plants to grow into crops such as wheat, and harvest them when they were ripe.

Farming produced more food than hunting and gathering. But until the 1800s, many people needed to work on farms to produce enough food for everyone.

▲ This woman is harvesting a rice crop in Nepal.

Cattle like these can be raised for meat or for their milk. ▼

Machines and science

About 250 years ago, farmers in wealthier countries started using machines to help them. The machines did the work of many people, which meant a few farmers could produce food for lots of other people. Many people could now do other jobs, such as manufacturing, instead of farming.

Scientists developed chemicals to help farmers produce more food. They also developed new kinds of plants and new breeds of animals.

Many farmers now use chemicals such as fertilizers, pesticides and herbicides to grow more crops. Fertilizers make the soil more fertile. Pesticides kill insects that harm crops, and herbicides kill weeds among the crops.

◄ Two combine harvesters in a huge wheat field.

Farming today

Today, in wealthy countries such as Britain and the USA, most people live in cities and rely on a few farmers in the countryside to grow their food.

But many people are worried about how their food is produced. Chemicals sprayed on crops can stay on the food we eat. They can also run into rivers and the water underground. New kinds of plants and new breeds of animals may upset the natural environment. Valuable soil is being lost or damaged.

Some people think we should look for ways of farming that do not damage the environment, or risk people's health and safety.

▲ Many animals are kept in small pens and cages, where they cannot move around or even lie down.

A balanced diet

Our bodies need a mixture of carbohydrates, fats, proteins, vitamins, minerals, water and fibre to stay healthy. These nutrients are found in different types of food, which we need to eat every day. This is called a balanced diet.

Many people in the world do not have a balanced diet, or cannot get enough food at all. There is enough food in the world to feed everyone, but not everyone can afford to buy it.

◀ People in Somalia wait for food to be given to them.

POOR DIETS

Over 2 billion people in the world do not have a balanced diet. Over 500 million people cannot get enough food at all.

Activity

FOOD DIARY

Write down a list of everything you eat and drink during one day.

Beside the food name, write down the nutrients it contains. You can look on the packaging to find the nutrients.

Are you eating a balanced diet?

Hamburgers contain meat, but many hamburgers contain only a few nutrients because the meat is poor quality. ▼

Types of food
The most important type of food is cereal grain, such as wheat, corn and rice. Grain is grown on half the world's farmland and provides many important nutrients.

Animals such as cattle, chickens and goats supply meat, eggs and milk. Meat also contains many nutrients, but it is more expensive than grains. Many people cannot afford to buy meat.

Animal feed

Cattle, sheep and other grazing animals eat grass. They turn grass into food that humans can eat, in the form of meat and milk.

But on some farms, cattle are fed grain to make them grow quicker and produce more meat. Grain is also fed to chickens, to make them grow quicker and produce more eggs.

In some parts of the world, the only food people can afford to buy for themselves is grain. But the grain is being fed to animals instead.

▲ Caged battery chickens being fed grains.

GRAIN FOOD

About 40 per cent of the world's grain is fed to animals.

CATTLE FARMING IN NAMIBIA

Namibia is a country in south-west Africa. It is very dry because there is little rain and it is very hot.

The soil is so poor in Namibia that only dry grass, bushes and trees can grow. It is not good enough to grow crops. The only type of farming is cattle. They are farmed for their meat.

There are over 2 million cattle on farms in Namibia, and only 1.4 million people. Each cow needs 15 hectares to find enough grass to eat. Only farmers with large farms make a good living. People with small areas of land struggle to raise enough cattle to feed their families.

Cattle in Namibia. ▼

The importance of soil

Soil contains living materials. Most living things depend on it for food. Plants draw up nutrients from soil through their roots. Animals eat the plants. When plants and animals die they decay and break down into the soil, which adds nutrients. This is called the soil cycle.

It takes between 3,000 and 12,000 years to make a new layer of soil for growing crops.

Ploughing a rice field in China. ▼

Soil erosion

Soil is being blown or washed away all the time. This is called erosion. Grass and trees help stop soil erosion because their roots keep the soil in place. Farming can increase soil erosion by destroying grass and trees.

Farming can destroy grass by overgrazing. This happens when too many animals feed on an area of grass, leaving the soil bare.

▲ Soil erosion in Malawi.

▲ New settlers in Guatemala cut down and burn trees to clear farmland.

Destroying trees

Farming destroys trees because people cut them down to make new farmland. This happened hundreds of years ago in countries such as Britain and the USA. Today it is happening in poorer countries, such as Brazil and Indonesia.

In tropical countries there are often heavy rains and the soil is thin. If forests have been cut down, the rain washes away the soil, leaving little for farmers to use.

SOIL EROSION

Every year, 10 million hectares of forest are cut down. Rain and wind erode 23,000 tonnes of soil.

Farming methods

Farming methods can also damage the soil. Ploughing loosens soil, so it is easily blown away. Heavy machines flatten the soil, squeezing out the air and water that plants need to survive. Chemical pesticides and fertilizers damage the soil by killing the living material in it.

Big machines damage the soil. They press it down so that air cannot get into it. ▼

TERRACED FARMING IN CAMEROON

Cameroon is a country in West Africa. The Kilum mountain forest is in the north-west of the country. The climate is cool and the soil is fertile.

As the population grows, the forest is cleared for farmland. To prevent soil erosion, flat terraces of soil are dug around the hillside.

▲ These farmers are digging flat terraces around a hillside, so the soil does not wash away. They are using an A-frame to check that the ground is level.

Protecting soil

Our food and farming depend on soil. So it is important that the way people farm does not erode the soil, or make it infertile.

Activity

SOIL EROSION TEST

1. Line four cardboard boxes with silver foil and cut a V-shape at one end of each box.

2. Fill three boxes with soil and the fourth with turf.

3. Smooth the surface of the first box, make furrows widthways across the second box and lengthways across the 3rd box.

4. Lift one end of each box 5 cm and put a bowl under the other end.

5. Sprinkle water over each box.

   Which box loses the most soil?

Box 4   Box 3   Box 2

Box1

Crops and animals

Crop farming is called arable farming. Crops are grown for food and for other materials, such as cotton.

The main food crops in the world are cereal grains and root crops. The other important crops are pulses, fruits and vegetables, soybeans, sugar-cane, nuts, cocoa beans, coffee and tea.

This farm grows both crops and animals. ▼

Activity

FARM QUESTIONNAIRE

Plan a visit to a farm near you. Prepare some questions for the farmer, such as:

1. What animals do you keep?

2. What crops do you grow?

3. Do you use fertilizers, pesticides or herbicides?

4. How is each building used?

5. How is each field used? Does this change every year?

Trace a map of the farm. Use the answers to your questions to show how each part of the farm is used.

Intensive crop farming

Where land is expensive, farmers grow as much as possible on an area of land. They grow the same crop in several big fields. They may grow the same crop every year. This is called monoculture.

Farmers plant special seeds that have been developed by scientists to grow bigger crops. Chemical fertilizers and pesticides are sprayed on crops.

The chemicals can pollute the water in rivers, and underground. They can also damage the soil by destroying the living material in it. Monocultures make the land less fertile.

▲ Farm workers spraying pesticides on fruit trees.

WORLD CROPS

Crops grow on 1.5 billion hectares of land around the world.

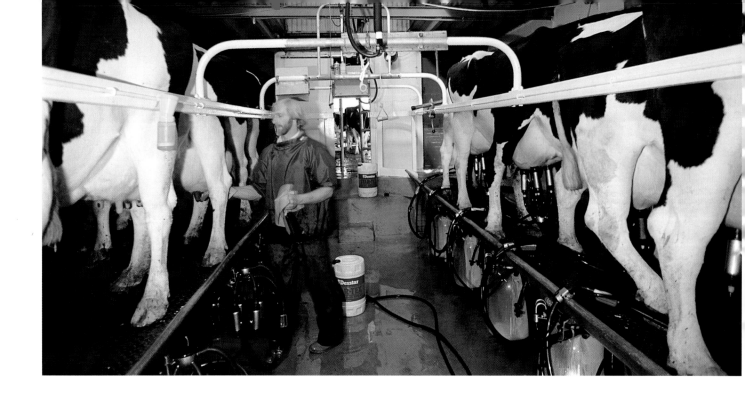

▲ Machines being used to milk cows.

Intensive animal farming

Animal farming is called livestock farming. Animals are farmed for food, and other materials such as wool. The main animals raised for food are cattle, chickens, goats, pigs and sheep.

On intensive farms, animals are kept in pens instead of in fields where they can roam around. Many cannot lie down or even turn around. They are fed grain so they grow quicker and produce more meat, eggs or milk.

Many people think that intensive farming is cruel to animals. It can also be dangerous. Animals on intensive farms are given medicines to prevent the spread of disease. These medicines could be passed to humans in the meat.

Animal waste

Intensive farms produce large amounts of waste from animals, called manure or slurry. Some slurry is used as a natural fertilizer. But some is washed into rivers. This pollutes the water.

One cow can produce 10 tonnes of manure in a year.

TRUE STORY

CHICKEN FARM

Michael Vine runs a small chicken farm in East Sussex, in England. He buys chicks when they are one day old and keeps them in sheds.

▲ These chicks are one day old.

Michael feeds the chickens a special grain mixture, which he buys from a shop. The feed makes the chickens grow more quickly than they would naturally. If necessary, Michael can add medicines to the chickens' water to stop disease. The chickens are killed when they are at least six weeks old and sold for meat.

These chickens are four weeks old. ▼

Michael has tried free-range farming, where the chickens wander outside, but it was too expensive. 'Some people aren't willing to pay more for the chickens. They want food to be as cheap as possible.'

GM foods

Plants, animals and people contain a mixture of different genes, which carry information about characteristics such as height and colour.

In the 1970s and 1980s, scientists discovered which genes carried particular information and how to move them between plants. This is called genetic engineering.

Scientists can now grow new species of plants that have the characteristics farmers need, such as growing bigger crops and resisting pests. Food from these crops is called genetically modified, or GM, food.

◀ A scientist working with plants.

◀ This boy's banana is an entirely natural fruit. Some people think that genetic engineering is dangerous and interferes too much with nature.

Dangers of GM foods

Many people are worried about GM foods. We do not know yet whether new species of plants might harm the environment. If they do, the plants would be difficult to control because they could breed with wild plants.

We do not know whether GM foods could be bad for our health. Some countries now label all GM foods clearly, so that people can choose whether to buy them or not.

A FOOD COMPANY

Monsanto is a large food company based in Missouri, in the USA. The company has spent a lot of money on scientific research into food plants. It has developed new species using genetic engineering, which grow bigger crops or resist pests.

Two of Monsanto's new plants are New Leaf potatoes and YieldGard corn. These resist insect attacks better than other types of potato or corn. Many of the company's plants are used and eaten all over the world.

Genetic engineering helps produce bigger crops. ▼

Losing variety

It is important to have a variety of different plants in the world. Scientists cannot make genes, they can only use ones from existing plants. Genetic engineering may mean fewer different types of plant species, because farmers will only want to grow food plants that produce big crops.

▲ Once plant species die out, they cannot be replaced.

Activity

Find out how many species of plants grow in your school grounds.

1. Make a square frame out of cardboard, measuring 1 metre by 1 metre.

2. Choose two different places in your school grounds where grass or plants grow, such as a playing field and a grass verge.

3. In each place, put the frame on the ground and count the number of different plants you find. What do you notice?

4. What would the plants need to allow more types to grow?

The future

In the last thirty years, people have become worried about how their food is farmed and the effect on the environment. Many people do not want to eat food from crops sprayed with pesticides, or from animals raised on intensive farms. They want food grown in ways that do not damage the environment. This is called organic farming.

Organic farmers do not use chemical pesticides or fertilizers, and they try not to cause pollution. They let animals wander outside some of the time, instead of keeping them in sheds all their lives.

More and more farmers are trying organic farming, because more people want organic food. Organic farmers have to follow strict rules about how they produce food.

These organic apples have been grown without chemical pesticides. ▶

AN ORGANIC FARM

Bill Brammer runs an organic farm in California, in the USA. He grows about sixty different types of fruit and vegetables on the farm.

Bill takes great care of the soil on the farm and uses only natural fertilizers to keep the soil fertile. He says: 'Our fields are fertilized with compost and rock minerals. We have found that if the soil and plants get balanced nutrients, we have fewer pest problems. We believe that because of our soil quality, our produce is more nutritious, has better flavour and lasts longer than non-organic produce.'

A quarter of the food from Bill's farm is sold in boxes to local people every week. They know that every box contains food grown organically and in season on the farm.

▲ A farmer spreading animal manure on the soil, to fertilize it naturally.

▲ Pigs on a mixed farm.

Mixed farming

Mixed farming is an older type of farming where animals and crops are raised on the same farm. Fields are given a rest from growing crops and grow grass instead. Animals in the fields eat the grass and their manure provides a natural fertilizer.

Each field grows a different crop each year. There would be more pests if the same crop was grown in a field every year. Many farmers are now trying mixed farming again, to improve the quality of their soil.

Making choices

We are all responsible for the way farming affects the environment. This is because the food we choose in the supermarket affects the way it is farmed. For example, if everybody bought only organic food, all farmers would have to change to organic farming because they wouldn't be able to sell anything else.

If we want to protect the environment, people's health and animal welfare, we need to make careful choices about the food we buy and eat.

Activity

MAKE SOME COMPOST

1. Ask an adult to help you cut two plastic bottles in half.
2. Fill one half with vegetable peelings and grass cuttings, fasten a cloth over the end with a rubber band and fix it inside the other half as shown in the diagram.
3. Fasten the top of the other bottle and make some holes to let in air.
4. Add water every day and watch the mixture turn into compost.

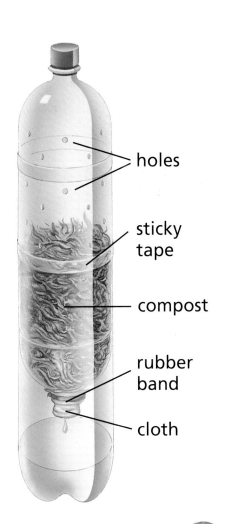

holes

sticky tape

compost

rubber band

cloth

Glossary

Balanced diet A mixture of different kinds of food and drink eaten every day, which provides the nutrients we need to stay healthy.

Billion A million millions.

Compost A mixture of rotten plants and animal material which is rich in nutrients and can help plants grow.

Diet The food we eat and drink every day.

Erosion Wearing away of the soil and the earth's surface.

Fertilizers Substances that make soil more fertile, or productive.

GM food Food grown from plants produced by genetic engineering. Particular genes are combined to make a new species of plant.

Harvest To gather grain or other crops.

Herbicides Chemicals that kill particular types of plants.

Intensive Producing a lot from a small area.

Manure Waste from animals.

Mixed farms Farms where animals and crops are grown.

Nutrients Things that feed plants, animals and people.

Pesticides Chemicals that kill pests, usually insects.

Root crops Vegetables that grow underground, such as potatoes.

Welfare A good state of health and happiness.

Further information

MUSIC
- Compose a 'rap' or musical piece to explore issues of food production
- Animal sounds

GEOGRAPHY
- Landforms and processes
- Human use of land
- Nature conservation
- Population density
- Environmental issues: e.g. erosion, pollution
- Differences in farming due to climate, soil and resources

HISTORY
- Changes in farming over time; including agricultural and industrial revolutions

ART & CRAFT
- Design a poster to promote organic food, conservation of soil or animal welfare, for local display

Topic Web

DESIGN AND TECHNOLOGY
- Construct an A frame to measure contours
- Make a compost bin

MATHS
- Measurement e.g. contours of land
- Compare prices of organic and non-organic foods

SCIENCE
- Ecosystems
- Biodiversity
- Food chains
- Nutrients and diet
- Soils
- Environmental issues: e.g. habitat loss, water pollution, loss of ecosystems, sustainability

ENGLISH
- Write letter to local supermarket to ask about organic food
- Write a 'newspaper article' on farming

Other books to read

Action for the Environment: Food for All by Chris Oxlade and Rufus Bellamy (Franklin Watts, 2004)

21st Century Debates: Genetics by Paul Dowswell (Hodder Wayland, 2002)

Earth's Changing Landscape: The Effects of Farming by Andrea Smith (Franklin Watts, 2003)

Earth Watch: Feeding the World by B. Walpole (Watts, 2000)

Health Matters: Food and Your Health by Jillian Powell (Hodder Wayland, 2002)

Life Files: Food Matters by Jillian Powell (Evans, 1998)

Saving our World: Genetically Modified Food by N. Hawkes (Franklin Watts, 2003)

Step-by-Step Geography: Farming and Industry (Franklin Watts, 2002)

Straightforward Science series: Food Chains & Plant Life by Peter Riley (Franklin Watts, 2003)

Sustainable World: Food and Farming by Rob Bowden (Hodder Wayland, 2003)

Talking Points: Animal Rights by Barbara James (Hodder Wayland, 2002)

Index